ARE YOU LOST OR FOUND?

RECOGNIZING THE WAKE UP CALL

A BOOK ON CHANGE, GROWTH AND SELF RESTORATION

SYLVESTER FADAL

authorHOUSE®

AuthorHouse™
1663 Liberty Drive, Suite 200
Bloomington, IN 47403
www.authorhouse.com
Phone: 1-800-839-8640

This book is a work of non-fiction. Unless otherwise noted, the author and the publisher make no explicit guarantees as to the accuracy of the information contained in this book and in some cases, names of people and places have been altered to protect their privacy.

First published by AuthorHouse 9/8/2008

ISBN: 978-1-4389-0306-4 (sc)
ISBN: 978-1-4389-0307-1 (hc)

Printed in the United States of America
Bloomington, Indiana

This book is printed on acid-free paper.

Dedicated to the outstanding individuals whose
unfolding lives inspired me to write this book.

CONTENTS

MY STORY

I was born into a household of honorable parents. Both were steadfast and upright at least to the best of my knowledge and based on the opinions of everyone that I have encountered in my years.

My father was a police officer for 22 years with a high level of integrity. I was not honorable by the least sense of the word in my opinion of my youth. I was simply put, obstinate. I was filled with a drive and highly forceful angst to be different. I hated rules. I was always willing to be on the opposite side of good principles.

From an ethical point of view, I was a consequential individual. I sort of knew very early a great deal about the principle of consequences and taking unreasonable risk. I was wise in my decisions when safety was a concern. In everything else, I didn't care. I was difficult. Sometimes too frank and truthful to those that knew me. My feedback was rarely sought unless the person wanted the absolute truth. I hated sleep because I thought it was a waste of time to play and break the rules. I often complained about going to bed.

At times I knew my parents were frustrated with my innate level of stubbornness. As luck would have it, my mother was very patient with me. My father took the old fashion approach and spanked me occasionally. Make that frequently when I broke the rules. It didn't matter to me. I feared being spanked but my desire for doing what I wanted overrode my concern for the consequences. The only time I wasn't acting on the extreme was when my safety was involved.

Because I was raised in a semi-religious home, I knew enough about God and heaven. I dreamt of heaven and the peace and quiet that I assumed came with it. I wanted to go to heaven but certainly was not in a rush to get there. I am still not in a rush despite my understanding and believe of Salvation and the grace of God. If I was young today I would be loaded with a long list of medications for attention deficit disorder (ADD). I could have been a classic case of the modern day ADD. Doctors perhaps could have been some of my best friends. I couldn't listen for more that a few minutes. Maybe seconds. My span of attention was short. I had a quick aptness for learning so I did well understanding and remembering things but my interest in any specific subject was minimal. I bored easy. At the age of 11,

I was sent off to a boarding school in line with the British model of education that my parents dearly believed in.

I approached the world with a desire to be myself and play by my rules of challenging the status quo. I violated most rules and accepted the strict consequences.

With time I started to realize my strength and weaknesses. I was a marshal for the disadvantaged. I was overly empathetic. I grieved easy. I was excessively emotional when I observed inequities. Perhaps one of my positives was and still is my empathy for the weak, the poor, and the disadvantaged. Most fights I got into were in defense of others that I thought couldn't defend themselves. I was willing to take the heat for others. I disliked the financial dichotomy between the rich and the poor. This breath of empathy started to change my person and my rebellious nature.

My life began to undergo a metamorphosis. I was clearly a typical case of one that was LOST. When I started to tap into my windows of opportunities and the repository of positive things that gave me satisfaction and expand on them, I became much calmer and cooperative. I became more content and confident. I learned to follow the rules. I found happiness in places when I never thought I would. I felt enriched. I refocused my energy to positive things and in no time developed a persona of "ultimate acceptability" whatever that means.

Today, I am proud to present myself as an example of a person who was completely "Lost" based on my analysis and that of close friends and family members. I changed into a "Found" being. I surround myself with things that impact me and the lives of others positively. I seek to please others (that truly need the assistance) and in the process, I gain satisfaction.

This book is simple but finitely valuable as it relates to gaining self-satisfaction and an upbeat attitude to life. It is a book on embracing change. Empirical to a point and fictional in some cases, the goal is to provide you with a factual and realistic depiction of how to transition from a "Lost" to a "Found" person.

I personally consider this book "a development journal" written with great passion and hope that my transformation and change experiences could positively impact or maybe change your life like it did mine. I hope you find it a resource to help you grow, expand your knowledge and embrace a new beginning in your personal or professional life.

Sylvester

PREAMBLE

ARE YOU LOST OR FOUND?
THE BREAST IRONING FACTUAL STORY

Deep in the valley of an African Country is a cultural trend that has transcended generations. Young girls are married off at the tender ages of between 12 and 15 depending on their level of physical development. To avoid possible early marriages or rape of their young daughters based on traditional culture, concerned mothers resort to breast ironing or flattening.

BREAST IRONING

Breast ironing is a form of body modification or unnatural sculpting practiced in parts of Cameroon, Africa. Mothers flatten pubescent girls' breasts in an attempt to make them less sexually attractive to men. This practice is believed to help prevent rape and early marriages. Tools such as grinding stones, pestles, wild leather belts, or heated objects are used to press or beat down the forming breasts. Local non-governmental organizations have over the years made plenary efforts to call attention to the practice in an attempt to put a stop to it. Despite the efforts and sporadic outcry against it, the practices remain. As crude and archaic as it sounds, most mothers practice the painful act of breast ironing out of love and protection for their young daughters.

This precaution sometimes does not stop some of these young girls from being forced into situations they can't prevent. In cases where pre-arranged early marriages can't be avoided due to early puberty and fast physical development, these young girls become unwilling spouses at very tender ages. In no time and with limited experience, they become mothers of new babies. As young mothers, they tackle the responsibilities of caring for their babies and husbands. Of importance though is the way these young girls learn to develop a commendable level of resilience in the long run.

With limited resources these young mothers would sometimes have to walk over two miles for basic amenities up to and including water that is fetched from a stream. With babies placed on their backs and wrapped up firmly with a piece of approximately 2 yards of plain cloth to ensure a balanced grip in an old-fashioned way of the modern day baby pack, the cloth is then tied into a knot in front of the mothers' bellies and repositioned to ensure a solid grip.

These mothers, having secured their babies on their back, would proceed to fold another piece of cloth into a small-sized circular shape and place it on their heads. In some sort of a strategic form, they will proceed to place a large bucket or container on their heads in preparation for the four-mile round-trip walk to get drinkable water from the stream or watercourse. At times, they repeated these trips twice daily. In a routine form, they also used the same approach in their trips to the market or other places of needs.

In addition to the babies on their back and heavy items placed on their heads, most women would carry additional items in both hands. They would need to stop literally and take a break if they needed to use their hands.

These girls with barely developed bodies and brains become completely independent from the guidance of their parents and within a short period, they develop and build outstanding levels of resiliency to life and the ability to cope with the situations they face. Despite these seemingly difficult lifestyles, some of them remain content within the situations they find themselves and are noted as some of the happiest set of people based on their level of satisfaction with life.

Proven over the years is that some of these women when taken out of their labor-intensive, difficult lifestyles and migrated to comfortable and developed environments, are better able to adapt and excel than

those raised under less strenuous, tedious, and difficult surroundings.

Why you might ask? The reality is, the ability of these young girls to overcome difficult times is their learned and ferocious volitional desires and willingness to succeed. They are raised to recognize the need to look to themselves for their failures rather than blaming everyone around them. They learned very early to embrace life as they find it and to embrace change as it comes. They realized very early that not everyone has a choice and for those that do, as long as the door has a knob, it is acceptable to open the door and embrace change or a new life of being a "Found" person.

PREFACE

For almost 10 years, I have spoken to captivated students and teams about the "Lost and Found" analogy. Here is how it all began. As an adjunct professor of undergraduate and graduate courses in Silicon Valley, California, I had the opportunity to help develop individuals and leaders in the hi-tech, biotech, and other varied industries. With time, my students and I developed a rapport of understanding and development that has shaped our lives positively. On occasions, we discussed issues of leadership, relationship, management and the complexities of leading and/or dealing with personal and professional life intricacies.

Personally, I gained an innate understanding of the concerns of these students as employees, managers, and leaders. I realized through shared discussions that most employees were likely to be unhappy with their jobs unless they develop a way to maintain a level of self-empowerment. One of the commonality of complaints raised by those surveyed and through feedback gained from personal discussions was that most employees joined their corporations with a high sense of commitment, enthusiasm and satisfaction and with time, lost their motivation and focus and literarily functioned as non-motivated employees driven solely by financial needs and or dependence.

Over the years I observed how some of these professionals took on higher levels of stress and anxiety over problems they couldn't control. To assist with strategies of addressing stress, I began to lecture my students on a concept known as "peaceful anxiety." Peaceful Anxiety simply means,

If you do not have the ability to change events and situations that impact your life, do not overreact to such situations.

While some level of stress and anxiety is acceptable, it is important to moderate our reaction especially if we have limited control over such situations. Regardless of how we react, events will naturally run their course so we must avoid placing ourselves in situations of ongoing discomfort that could trigger other negative effects. We must learn to immediately let go of our negative thoughts and actions relating to the issues that are not within our immediate control. As we develop the ability to control our reactions to problems or issues outside our realms of control, we begin to develop a higher sense of peace.

In 2002, having decided to migrate this knowledge and these experiences into a book, I commenced a survey focused on finding out why people, regardless of their levels of motivation, satisfaction and commitment upon joining a corporation or commencing a new project, gradually lost their zeal over time. Armed with a set of questions, I began to interview undergraduate and graduate students with professional careers ranging from information technology to top-level positions in management and leadership roles of all kinds. Responses were quantified and presented in a descriptive statistical layout alongside interesting narrative responses as presented unedited in a section of this empowerment book. My overall findings lead to this book being titled **Are You Lost or Found?**

PART ONE

CHAPTER 1

ARE YOU LOST OR FOUND?

Most corporations have primarily, two kinds of employees, the "Lost" and the "Found." To immediately find out where you belong, you can take the Lost or Found Survey listed under Exhibit 1

LOST OR FOUND SURVEY RESULTS

My research found that over 62% of the people interviewed were Lost while 26% were Found. The additional 12% were noted as the "Shiftless" group who were to an extent devoid of ambition or purpose but were not completely Lost. These findings lead to an expansion of the research to find out why so many individuals felt Lost. The follow up research regarding those who felt they were mostly lost in their workplaces culminated in the design of a follow up survey that asked participants who they would rather have as a boss. The results and narratives alongside additional information relating to the survey are presented in chapter 9.

THE LOST

The "Lost" employees are sometimes easy to identify as indicated by their actions, behaviors, morale levels, resistance to anything that shifts their comfort zones, unwillingness to accept responsibility, a quick aptness to blaming others, hemorrhagic tendencies and a propensity to complain daily, and acting like endangered species among others.

Some basic traits of a "Lost" employee are:
Always Fearful
Easily Frustrated
Complacent
Non-Motivated
Silo-Driven (Loner)
Poor Attitude
Hates Change
Negative
Combative
Frequent Absenteeism
Embrace Presenteeism

Non-Team Player

Highly Secretive

Frequent Complainer

Self-Demotivator

Negative Proclivity

Quick Starter and Non-Finisher

Not-My-Job Slogans

THE FOUND

On the other end are the "Found." These are those that embrace change, take responsibilities for their actions, take initiatives, understand the values of team work, follow directions effectively, self-motivate, and understand the fundamentals of organizational behaviors up to and including the intricacies of organizational systems.

Typical traits of the "Found" employee are:

Embraces Change

Embraces Challenges

Builds Satisfaction

Team Oriented

Self-Motivated

Passionate

Assertive

Visionary

Positive Energy

Ambitious

Self-Motivators

Drivers

Team-Oriented

Great Followers

Great Leaders

Selective Starters and Great Finishers

It is easier to fall into the "Lost" pile than the "Found" pile and as such, this book is written in the most basic yet practical sense, to hopefully, help you develop an awareness of your leaning and how to develop an attitude of being a "Found" employee and person as it relates to your personal life.

Remember that not getting what you want is sometimes
a wonderful stroke of luck.
Dalai Lama

CHAPTER 2

WHERE DO YOU BELONG? WHERE WOULD YOUR TEAMMATES OR FRIENDS CLASSIFY YOU?

If your coworkers or friends were asked to classify you into the Lost or Found category, based on the parameters presented in Chapter One, where do you realistically believe you would fall? Based on long-range research, conducting surveys with working professionals, most individuals were either "Lost" or "Found." Our research identified some individuals who fell in the middle ground. We classified them as Hoverers or Shiftless.

Professionally, while some employees have found ways to embrace the complex realities of work and devised ways to fit in among the "Found," some remain completely "Lost" and confused from day to day. **They go to work and function in a relatively self-created stressful form and literally complain about prevailing and changing actions.** Yet in the midst of their self-generated unhappiness, they take comfort in blaming others and seeking validations for their level of dissatisfaction at work or in their personal lives. Did you know prior to this survey if you were "Lost or Found?" Prior to implementing the survey on some individuals, they were able to easily identify where they belong professionally and personally. Regardless of your section, the information laid out in this book, orchestrated by the experiences of professionals like you, will help you identify strategies to forever be a "Found" person.

KNOW YOUR BOUNDARIES

What are your functional boundaries? When all else fails, do you find ways to place blame on others? Do you view depression and sadness as a way to address an unachieved goal? It is important to avoid being depressed. Don't take your failure as a weakness or an opportunity to blame others. Rather, you should embrace your failure as a learning process and commend yourself for trying. Be resolute in your effort to try again, embrace change and do what is right for your personal growth. Acknowledge your failure as a developmental step.

At a graduation, a speaker spoke of some great students who knew their boundaries.

He gave a specific example of a student he thought was great. The student he noted wanted to be a Physical Therapist, held a strong passion for that line of work and was excited about one day being called a certified Physical Therapist.

The student studied hard and was dedicated to his goal.

Somewhere along the line, as part of his hands-on internship training the student was assigned to an outpatient clinic and a hospital on a 6-month study. In the role, the student worked with patients in pain and those who just had surgeries. The student quickly realized his boundaries and that his empathy for the sick and sympathy for those in pain not only brought him close to tears often, but also created a deep, unpleasing emotion within him. It was not his calling. His boundary was clear. Despite the student's passion and desire to be a Physical Therapist, he was not prepared for the realities of the job.

Rather than continue in a field filled with pain and emotional issues, the student made a decision and embraced a new career where he went on to touch the lives of thousands of people, earning a doctorate in business administration and influencing the future of most of his students as it relates to understanding boundaries and embracing change. This student,

the speaker noted, was a great student who knew his boundaries and was willing to lose 14 months of his life to ensure a bright and fulfilling future.

I am that student.

If you fail in your pursuit, always remember one important point, at least you tried. The architecture behind every success is the willingness to try to embrace a level of risk. Remember your independence of action, your freedom of choice and your self-esteem can't be stolen because you failed while trying. It is better to try and not succeed than not to try at all. The hidden mechanism behind every success is the successive desire to embrace smart work with a willingness to accept progress satisfaction or failure at every level, accompanied with a self-accomplishment motto.

Failure sometimes is a good thing. It is an accomplishment because it teaches you what not to do. It is an effective process of elimination. It makes you work harder and smarter with a higher volitional focus to succeed. It is an effective learning process. Hard work is good. But be sure you love what you do because if you don't, it will be difficult to devote your focus and energy to it in the long run. You can't be bored doing something you truly love.

If you have a "Lost" personality, you are probably stuck in one of the following:

  a. Taking your job too seriously,
  b. Doing something you don't enjoy,

c. Not giving to charity or lack of any level of altruism,

d. Not engaged in extracurricular activities that could bring you satisfaction,

e. Not efficiently developing yourself or others with a truly caring mind, and

f. Bored at what you do and feel like you are at a dead-end road.

If any of these stagnation tendencies apply to your current situation, perhaps it is time to make a change.

CHAPTER 3

LET YOUR CONSCIENCE JUDGE YOUR LEVEL OF PERSONAL ACTS.

Are you engaged in activities or works that bring you personal satisfaction and a level of salient joy? The strength inherently possessed by the "Found" is gained by their distinctive aptness for embracing change and finding satisfaction at all times, even in unconventional situations typically considered stressful grounds. If you are not easily pleased with the actions you have been engaged in for years, it is perhaps time to build a symbiotic ability to do what your conscience tells you is right, spiritually, ethically, legally, and philanthropically. Shift your focus to helping the needy and the under-privileged. Reach out to someone else or your hidden true desires and not what society expects from you. You are yourself so be You. It is not enough to say you are not in a position to assist others. It is easier to justify inability than ability.

You can be an inspiration to others intrinsically or tangibly. It doesn't matter what your personal achievements are, if you have not (a) truly worked for your wealth, (b) learned to give and reach out to the disadvantaged at some level, (c) developed a level of discipline and focus as it relates to your sense of self and, (d) impacted something of value somehow or somewhere, you have failed. John Wesley, an 18th-century Anglican clergyman and well regarded Christian theologian said it best with the following words:

Work all you can
Save all you can
Give all you can

Ask yourself if you have truly done your best, working all you can, saving all you can and, giving selflessly?

John Wesley's recommendation, though not popularly recognized in the secular world, has been adopted knowingly or un-intentionally by some of the wealthiest and generous Americans such as Warren Buffet, Oprah Winfrey and, Bill Gates among others in their unfailing desires to give to the underprivileged. You may simply say, "Oh, they are rich beyond measures and can afford to do just that." Not true! Those that are prone to giving, when they can barely afford to make ends meet, are more likely to maintain the same appropriateness of reasoning and generosity when they become rich or wealthy. There have been individuals with barely enough to meet their personal needs; who religiously devote time and money to those that are poor and needing much more support to ensure daily subsistence. It is a mindset that is often adopted by the "Found," a giving attitude that ultimately generates an innate level of satisfaction and joy that has no relationship to wealth or status. Think about this for a moment! Do those that religiously give, end up poorer than others? No, they don't. They have a higher level of satisfaction and contentment than those that abhor giving. They gain more satisfaction from giving to others and supporting the underprivileged.

Today, as you read this book, take the first step to shifting into the "Found" column or affecting the life of someone else. Give. Just give or simply try doing something different but valuable for someone else. Give with a heart of joy and satisfaction. It does not have to be monetary. Just give and watch the circle of your satisfaction fill up fast.

FEAR

Why do you think you are stuck in the "Lost" circle you find yourself in daily regardless of your financial situation? Are you afraid of change? Do you find yourself in a perpetual state of fear? It is important to note that the underpinning outcome of fear is never positive but always an unnecessary stagnation of personal and professional development. It is acceptable to have what is called "legitimate concern" due to prevailing life situations. When concerns are baseless and bounding to a state of an inability to control ones unreasonable level of constant fear, it becomes an illness.

He is noted as a gifted and talented competitor that illuminated ardent baseball fans with his athletic ability. He orchestrated the 1987 and 1991 championship victories of the Minnesota Twins. A man of integrity and reliability, he rejected bigger contracts from other teams to remain with the Twins for his entire career out of loyalty. Kirby Puckett, who died suddenly in 2006, will always be remembered for among other things, his ability to control and manage his fears. When his career ended abruptly in 1996 when he was diagnosed with glaucoma, he remained positive and never gave in to the fear of complex life intricacies because of the sudden end to his baseball career.

During his induction into the Baseball Hall of Fame in 2001, he spoke of his difficult upbringing and how the desire to play professional baseball kept him focused and deterred him from engaging in the common activities of his neighborhood such as drugs and gangs.

Do not let fear compromise your happiness. You only live once and your life belongs to you. Ephesians 4:1 says it clearly, noting that we must "walk worthy of the calling with which [we] were called." Kirby Puckett's passion to become a professional baseball player was subject to temptation many times. He never gave in to the temptations for fear of rejection. There are people across the world filled with varied fear up to and including the fear of progressively moving on to anything that takes them out of the realms of their comfort zones. This kind of fear-generated stress must be let go immediately.

STRESS

Stress is an agonizing concern that could be emotional. Often generated by external or internal, self-orchestrated influences and stimuli, it is to a great extent, controllable. The simplest approach is to develop a mindset that if something is not going to affect your life the next day, a week or a month later, let go of the concern immediately. There is no point stressing for weeks, months or sometimes years, before letting go. If external factors are the generators of ones stress, it is important to seek and change the factors or environment as soon as possible. If the driving factors of the stress are outside the realms of ones control, don't embrace the stress of it. Move on. Be as it may, it is unnecessary to stress about something outside one's control.

ARE YOU AFRAID?

People hate change and the unknown. To an extent, this is normal. They gravitate to what they know best and have control over. This is the comfort zone syndrome. The need to remain in one's comfort zone is the main driver of resistance to change. Most individuals justify their resistance to change by words such as:

I have done it this way too long and can't change now

Well that's just who I am. Is too late to change
Change is not in my nature
Someday things will change around me and conform to
my style.

You can and must seek to break the alignment to being "Lost." The "Lost" are filled with sadness and high levels of dissatisfaction in their daily lives, which permeates their entire activities. Don't be one of those that are afraid to let go of it all. Be quick to move on to something else that will bring you the greater good of life's satisfaction.

SOUL SEARCHING/HEALING

The infinite wisdom of finding self-satisfaction is to search within one's soul. As you read through this simple but yet pragmatic handbook, it is important to know that it doesn't matter (a) who you are, (b) what you do, (c) who has offended you, or (d) how bad your boss or coworkers are. What is important is that you let go of needless stress and devise means to start empowering your inner self. Restore your soul and let go of all the sadness and pain. Embrace a new life filled with joy, satisfaction, forgiveness and a conviction that you will seek the best out of every opportunity or disappointment that may come your way. Be quick to forgive and fast to recognize others. These are characteristics that will enhance your personal growth and move you into the "Found" section.

DON'T BE BOUND BY A BELIEF SYSTEM

Sometimes, our biggest or strongest obstacle is nothing else but our personal belief system and ways of thinking. If you stop expanding your learning and visionary reasoning, you could stagnate your growth. I typically use the analogy of my factual experience with my plants.

In 1998 I received two small sized plants. One was about a foot tall and the other nine inches tall. I placed them by my window so they could get some sunlight. Every two days, I watered them. With time, they grew and the need arose to repot the plants. I repotted the smaller plant and watched it grow to over 3 feet before I started pruning it. The initial taller plant remained stagnated and as I failed to repot it, it remains stunted in growth till this day.

With my eyes, I learned the effect of creating a bigger and wider compass and space to encourage growth. In other words, avoid being bound by a belief system or lack of dreams and opportunities that could lead to complete dysfunction and stagnation of your growth.

Don't willingly create an avoidance of things that may be great for you because your views on such things hinder your ability to see the gold within the dirt.

He was nicknamed "Bobby milk" in view of his pale complexion. Lonely and shy with a passion for reading, he conquered his timidity and rose to become one of today's most accomplished Hollywood actors.

He is arguably a great actor whose feeble beginning is unknown to most because of his breathtaking persona and amazing acting ability. If he can transform from a shy, timid and quiet young boy to playing some of the most entertaining and challenging roles in movies such as Mean Streets, The Godfather, Taxi Driver, The Deer Hunter, Raging Bull, among others, you can do it in your chosen field. With an academy award and other accomplishments, there is no better person to present as one that have successfully dug the gold out of his humble beginning than Robert De Niro.

Don't spend your life being bound by a belief system unless it is positive to your overall life. Be set free from your negative infirmities by a positive conviction of your mind. However, in your effort to embrace your newfound freedom of the mind, don't be in a rush. Apply a step-by-step approach to the change. Recognize each milestone that moves you forward. Strategically avoid those that continue to nibble at you and don't support your positive change.

SETTING YOURSELF FREE

To gain personal freedom, you must take a daily convictional approach to life. The freedom to succeed in your life both personal and professional depends on you. If you are truly ready, you should be willing to say, "regardless of what goes on in my life":

I will be gracious;

I will strive to live my dream;

I will rejoice with all I have regardless of my experiences good or bad;

I will forget my losses and develop new dreams;

I will get in the game of self-accomplishment and satisfaction;

I will cast away the broken hearts;

I will cast away the pain of work, failed relationships, heartbreaks, bad bosses or whatever brings me pain;

I will forever be in charge of my life and be happy.

Having said the above, you are on your way to:

Casting away the fear of non-acceptance;

Doing what brings you valid, righteous and balanced happiness;

Canceling the poor therapeutic treatments,

Moving on to great things;

Controlling your mindset by your actions and not others;

Living a gracious life;

Letting self-freedom and empowerment reign in you and embracing the "EXIT" sign to greater and better things in life.

CHAPTER 4

BE RESILIENT IN YOUR PURSUIT AND SATISFACTION

Tiger Woods has won some of the most competitive and dramatic tournaments in his amazing professional golf career. The bottom line mechanism orchestrating his success is his astonishing level of resilience and consistency, driven by his volitional conviction that he could achieve whatever he sets his mind. Unknown to most but yet a Guinness book of world record holder, is the fact that he has the record for qualifying for the most consecutive tournaments at 142 over a seven year span. This commendable achievement beats that of any living or dead player in the history of the United States or World of professional golf.

TIGER WOODS' RESILIENCY

When Tiger lost his father who he identified as his coach, best friend, and mentor, he went through a phase of pain and loss of motivation to continue to play golf. In his words, he said, "The hardest thing for me to do was play golf." Tiger described the death of his father as devastating and too painful to bear, saying, "My dad was my best friend and greatest role model." Upon return to professional golf after the death of his father, he missed the cut.

After missing the cut in a major tournament, which of course, created uproar in the golf world, the amazing ability of Tiger to overcome difficult life experiences was illuminated. He rebounded and won six tournaments in a row starting with the British Open through the month of October 2006. He ended the year with eight PGA Tour victories in 2006. An exceptional year by all standards, Wood's resiliency and ability to overcome difficult life situations with an amazing sense of focus, drive, and dedication was proven.

Today, as you read through this book, you may not have the outstanding competencies to be Tiger Woods. In every individual is the hidden innate ability and distinctive strength to excel amazingly when the right career or environment is found. If you are not in the career you truly desire, make one of two choices, (a) make a change as soon as reasonably feasible or (b) make the environment you find yourself the best it can be, by applying the focus and desire to succeed in any and all situations, using some or all of the strategies below.

COMMUNICATION

Perhaps the most common error of most individuals is the misunderstanding of the word communication. It is so broad "a word" that Alice Fadal once said "Communication knows no language if used wisely and appropriately...It can open or close doors and careers depending on how well it is used." According to Anne Cetas (2006) "Experts tell us that the average person speaks enough to fill 20 single-spaced, typewritten pages every day. This means our mouths crank out enough words to fill 2 books of 300 pages each month, 24 books each year, and 1,200 books in 50 years of speaking. Thanks to phones, voicemail, and face-to-face conversations, words comprise a large part of our lives. So the words we use are very important."

SOLILOQUY

The "Found" communicate frequently intra-personally. This is "soliloquy." Some call it self-talk. A great behavior molding strategy if used correctly, those in the "Found" column typically maintain a level of positivism in self-talk in view of its strong influence on attitude. The "Lost" typically self-talk themselves to a state of negativity that their attitude and actions become regressive to a state that no one wants to be around them. This lifestyle of ongoing negative self-talk often leads to high degree of stress, depression, frustration, and possibly suicide, career disengagement, low morale, and poor performance, among other illnesses. To engage others and communicate effectively, one must first learn to communicate intra-personally, effectively. This is the foundation of communication. Other important communication strategies used by those with "Found" characteristics are nonverbal effective techniques such as:

FACIAL

Communication, reflected positively or negatively through facial expression. It is important to master the act of pictographic communication of ensuring that your facial expression reflects, validates and supports your message. If you need to practice in front of the mirror, so be it. This skill is perhaps one of the most important face-to-face communication practices today and is most commonly mastered by those with the "Found" attitude.

CHOICE OF WORDS

Another important aspect of communication not frequently discussed is the "choice of words" aspect. Most experts over the years have failed to embrace this hidden innate value that choice of words adds to effective communication. For years, I was locked in a struggle of unintentional negative "choice of words" communication strategy. Even when I was in support of an idea, I often started comments with words such as "But" "You know what" "No" "I believe" "Really" "Why don't you." These words were typical effective communication disasters and regardless of how positive I intended, my choice of words portrayed and carried negative or non-supportive intents. With a conditional and intentional change effort, I learned to start with words such as "Great" "Absolutely" "Yes" "Definitely" "Sounds good" and so on. Regardless if I am not in support of an idea, I have learned to start off with a positive word.

INTONATION

One's tone and interaction style could influence the freedom of others to want to speak up. Applying basic protocol to avoid being condescending, rude, and discouraging is of utmost importance. Your intent may be good but your tone may not reflect that. You will not be evaluated based on your intent but how it is received. If your intonation is viewed negatively, it could be viewed as being insulting. It is important to learn to package the essence of ones message so it is captured accurately with respect for the rights of others and recognition of their person and/or viewpoints. Please apply common courtesy when giving feedback, input or simply contributing to a discussion. In the words of Whitney Young (1921 – 1971), "The truth is that there is nothing noble in being superior to somebody else. The only real nobility is in being superior to your former self."

FRIENDSHIP

A well-developed, mutual and balanced-oriented friendship is perhaps the most powerful motivator of humans as it relates to building self worth and growth. The circle of friends or non-friends thereof, dictates the ability of individuals to overcome periodic doom loops and maintain steady growth. Friends play different roles in one's life. Depending on where you are and your new direction or focus, it is important to develop and maintain the friends that would genuinely help you achieve your goals because; they truly want to see you succeed. Some friends are nibblers. They take and seek assistance non-stop and give nothing in return. It is important to identify your circle of friends to analyze the value they bring to your life. If their roles create a negative influence, it is perhaps time to reevaluate the friendship and its overall purpose.

PERSONALITY

Personality is a trait that could make or break a person regardless of education, wealth, or status. It is important to understand one's own personality and the way it is viewed from the eyes of others. If one's personality is positive, maintain it. If it is not yielding the desired results, make attempts to change or improve it. It is not okay to say it is just your personality. Because a style, behavior or attitude has been developed and mastered by an individual doesn't make it right if it impedes the ability of the person to maintain a positive, respectful relationship with others personally or professionally. If your personality doesn't fit or reflect the goals, values and relationships you seek, change it.

CHAPTER 5

INDIVIDUAL STRENGTHENING

Those in the "Found" section are skilled at establishing goals as it relates to building satisfaction in their personal and professional lives. They strive for ways to increase their growth and are cognizant of the fact that we don't live in a perfect world and they avoid seeking perfection in terms of people's actions. No organization regardless of its attempt to achieve excellence can achieve perfection in all areas. In place of expecting perfection from others or their companies, the "Found" seek ways to give and exert positive vibes and energy. They are altruistic and have realized that it is:

- An energy builder,
- Helps develop an inner level of satisfaction driven by the selfless, positive and realistic concern for others,
- Breed freedom in all ways,
- Reduces stress,
- Reduces the need to blame others,
- Helps build great character,
- Helps develop a gifting nature,
- Creates an autonomy from negative thoughts,
- Grows ones ability as it relates to wisdom to make the right decision at difficult times.

EMOTIONAL STRENGTHENING

To maintain a strong level of emotional control, the "Found" understand that change will happen. They don't continuously seek a comfort zone realizing that it is a downtrodden way to emotional circular discontentment. The "Found" are quick to understand the difference between (a) Compassion, (b) Love, and (c) Mercy.

COMPASSION

This entails the ability to care sympathetically for the pain and suffering of others. This is a good trait to have. It is also the symbiotic ability to want to give aid, support and give mercy to the needy, the poor, displaced, and those in states of misfortune.

ANGELINA JOLIE

Angelina Jolie is perhaps known and criticized by some for her most erratic behavior than for her humanitarian greatness in supporting the poor. She is arguably one of the most gifted actresses in Hollywood though she may not possess the best records in box office hits. Her personal accomplishments or lifestyle has no relevance here. What matters is her positive sense-of-self and personal level of satisfaction and joy, gained from her compassion for the underprivileged. This is what she is most respected for. What places her in the "Found" section is her incontestable ability to show innate and truthful compassion towards the needy. In this regard, she is an amazing human being. Before the new Hollywood fad to reach out to people in developing countries, she unglamorously and single-handedly commissioned herself to provide to those that would otherwise never have the opportunity for the most basic amenities of life.

Today, as you read this motivational, change-driven and empowerment book, you may have concerns of a:

- Failing marriage
- Lost or unstable job
- Financial struggles
- Unsupportive boss
- Difficult life situations
- Sick family members
- Sense of overall failure among others.

These may be issues of concern. They may be overwhelming problems right now to you. However, no problem, regardless of its magnitude is worth the total breakdown of one's life even before it begins. This is the situation faced by millions of poor children and families worldwide. To those in the remote villages in Cambodia, Kenya, Ethiopia, China and other third world countries, your situation will be considered a blessing. Why? Because you have options filled with potential opportunities. These poor families on the other hand, have little or no options. They lack the basic needs of life such as drinkable water, transportation, shelter or food and are willing to embark on a 5-mile trip to get basic needs such as water or food. Many poor children worldwide rely on the grace that is only provided by God and people like Angelina Jolie, Oprah Winfrey and Bill Gates among others.

Angelina Jolie recognized years ago, against all odds and without any glamour that the foundation of personal satisfaction rests in giving, supporting, having compassion, showing love and having mercy on others. She is a blessing to millions of orphans and she is fully admired for her philanthropic work. No wonder, she is a well-commended United Nations Goodwill Ambassador.

LOVE

In modern day, most have forgotten the true meaning of love. Those that remain in the "Found" category hold on to this categorical base of identifying love as the innate caring of a person based on personal or familial ties. While those in the "Lost" section seek love from others frequently, those in the "Found" section strive and passionately aspire to give love by first holistically loving themselves.

ANALYZING LOVE

Maintaining an intense attraction must be from the heart. A baseless intent attraction to another based solely on a selfish sexual or financial desire is not love. It must be a selfless desire to care for others. Mother Theresa lived her life giving and providing a true, sympathetic level of love to others for their own joy. She sacrificed her needs to ensure that others received a deep level of tenderness towards humankind. This altruistic nature and ability to care for others without a selfish interest is what defines love.

To be "Found" and to avoid being "Lost" one must begin to build a true sense of love from within, for our professional and personal connections regardless of what we expect to get in return. Rather than criticize, seek the positive aspect to all situations. Rather than gossip negatively about issues, situations, or people, praise one another. Rather than seek personal gain, give to those that least expect it but need it most. Rather than complain about your company, boss, projects, parents, siblings, leaders and money among others, reverse your actions and recognize the hidden lights behind the things that appear negative to you. Love for the selfless joy of it. **Gary Mortara**, a compassionate pastor, well renowned television preacher in Northern California and author of one of the most empowering faith based and leadership book for men, titled "**Be A Man**" once said, "A heart full of love knows no darkness."

MERCY

There is an old saying that "true failure is the failure to try." Having mercy requires a deep, kind, compassionate desire to treat others well. It is a holistic "disposition to be forgiving and kind" says the Webster's II New Riverside University Dictionary. How often do you practice the act of mercy? While we are quick to seeking grace and mercy from others, let's try giving in return. Reach out to those that have failed you when you needed them most. Grant mercy to those that disappointed you the most. At the end, enjoy the reward. Your grace and mercy towards others is a rewarding trait of the "Found."

VACUUM/NEGATIVE SELF SEIZURE

It is better to believe in a piece of stone than not to believe in anything at all. Some "Lost" individuals build up a level of negativity to a point where they "develop a sense of contentment" about "feeling bad always." In other words, they have reached a point of acceptance that it is alright to be negative all the time. They criticize everything they are in contact with. Their responses typically start with the word "NO" even with intents to respond positively. Yet, they expect to live a complete life of fulfillment. Avoid being in a vacuum. Practice the strategies of the "Found." Restructure your mind to think and react positively at all times and see the wonders of positivism overtake your life, reflect in your actions and exhume in your color.

Do little things with great love
Mother Theresa

CHAPTER 6

AVOID PERCENTILE NIBBLING (PEOPLE PRISONER)

Being a people prisoner is the continuous conscious need to please everybody at all times. Those that remain in the "Found" sections have volitional abilities to recognize the negative effects of being a people prisoner and devoid themselves of all such actions. They understand that one can't possibly please everybody at all times. They create a balance of knowing when to please others and when to objectively say no, and focus on their own needs. They have realized that the greatest development that breeds internal growth is, understanding the balance of giving and getting. Satisfaction and joy is the ability to delineate when to, and when not to, get influenced by external environmental perceptual factors or irrelevant influences.

THE GOPHER SYMDROME

Remember to keep track of your windows of existence and the best things and experiences of your life. They matter just as much as the future you seek. If you are feeling nibbled by situations, problems, and issues or factors that you can't control, you probably are and should immediately strive to replenish the circle of your loss. Don't get eaten from the inside out like a tree that looks great on the outside only to suddenly drop dead having been eaten up by a Gopher. A gopher is a short-tailed burrowing ground squirrel that eats trees from the inside out.

Over the years, I have observed people of great virtues react in self-defeatist ways due to sudden negative real life situations or experiences. You shouldn't. Remember that when a door closes, there is always a knob on the other side to open a new door to many exciting and challenging opportunities. Don't let it slip by you.

No matter what you do, people will either be pleased or displeased. It is not your responsibility to satisfy everyone. Avoid the urge to seek external acceptance at all times and simply follow the directions that fit your professional and personal development. Seek what creates the most balance between your needs and that of those/things that matter most to you. Be accountable to yourself, family, religion, work and other things of importance.

CHANGE AND CONTROL - THE BUTTE'
STRATEGY

Sometimes in our lives, things go wrong. That is a natural life phenomenon. It is nothing personal to you as a person. If all else fails and there is no sign of a bright future in the midst of your environs, it is acceptable to implement a complete transformational change towards a new direction to life just like a butterfly that could completely abandon its cocoon.

TIME

Most people discard the value of personal time and see no need to track its usage. Reality is, tracking the value of your time is a highly valuable habit. Move on quickly and remember that you have been blessed beyond measures. You have been endowed with the kindness of God and that per se is whole. Accept your situation as a new admirable level of growth. Recognize that sometimes your plans are just that, "plans" and are out of your hands. Be willing to embrace the change that comes on to you.

HAVE A DEVOTIONAL MOMENT (DM)

This is your time to reflect and recoup daily. You should have at least 3 DMs per day. This is a time to reflect on what works, what doesn't, your daily experiences, your work or life progress as it relates to that specific day. It is important to ask yourself how your daily actions support your overall goals. It must be a one-on-one session with you. This can be achieved while taking a private walk, spending a private time in the bathroom or simply a place where you can talk to yourself. Great individuals like Mahatma

Gandhi, Mother Theresa, and Dalai Lama all recognized the value, joy, development and ultimately, personal satisfaction that accompany that special, private devotional moment spent with oneself.

The mind is only as great as the positivism that feeds it

PART TWO

ARE YOU LOST OR FOUND?
THE PERCENTILE THEORY ANALOGY

CHAPTER 7

A BROKEN HEART
A FICTIONAL DEPICTION OF CORPORATE NIBBLING

The ultimate toll is hours away. Finally, the stress of the world and its imperfections is about to take the life of someone who has lived a life of pure perfection. Those who knew her well can feel the weight of the impending act. There is nothing left but an empty shell that houses a completely nibbled body that was once admired by most. Sadness has taken over Sophie who once possessed zeal of energy, life appreciation and created an atmosphere of ultimate joy.

Almost everyone is sad to see Sophie who grew up with a desire to succeed get torn down by the corporations she cherished and served dedicatedly. The actions of unskilled and uncaring managers who failed to see the value of empowering adults and treating them as capable individuals was set to claim the life of one of its own.

How did it all happen? How did Sophie get eaten up so badly by her corporation? What could have gone wrong? These are simply questions being asked by those who never saw it coming. This is one of those times when tears alone couldn't resolve a belated broken heart, spirit and soul. Sometimes, the impact of sadness created by the poor life experiences of individuals could be so overwhelming that every soul grieves for those that are nibbled to potential suicide.

Sophie Duze was born into an average family with simple but firm life principles such as maintaining (a) passion for hard work, (b) mutual respect for all, (c) willingness to succeed, (d) recognition and observance of individual pride and most important, (e) life nurtured by honesty and truth. Sophie's father Blake Duze was a hard workingman with a humble background and intentness to ensure that his family lived a decent and honorable life. Sophie's mother Allyxis was an anchor that held the family to the principles agreed upon by the Duze family. She also had a humble beginning and was raised to be gracious regardless of the situation in which she found herself.

Together, the Duze family practiced the doctrine of partnership based on mutual support, a caring for each other and the needy, a spiritual life dedicated to the works of God, a giving attitude that ultimately encourages and empowers others and a desire to impact the community in which they lived. Sophie is destined to die unless a miracle happens. She has no desire to live and on the brink of suicide. Quite frankly, nothing within her indicates nor justifies a need for continued existence. She has experienced a typical case of the percentile game that affects millions of people in the world today. Corporations (including churches and similar institutions alike) and people are contributors to the percentile game. To understand this fictional depiction of the Lost or Found Book and the extensive analogy used in it, you will have to understand the percentile theory and its devastating effect on people in their personal or professional lives.

CHAPTER 8

WHAT IS THE PERCENTILE GAME?

PERCENTILE THEORY: ORGANIZATIONAL GAME

In June of 1994, Sophie Duze graduated from an Ivy League college with an MBA at the age of 23 and was immediately recruited into one of the Fortune 100 corporations as a Business Analyst. Raised in Miami, Florida and schooled in the State of Massachusetts, a few months before her graduation, she was interviewed on campus, flown to California twice to interview as a business analyst with the corporation that ultimately hired her. She relocated approximately 2500 miles to California and began a new life as a professional. She was pleased, and life to her was good. Sophie entrusted herself into her work and had no sense of loneliness. With time, she began to learn the complexities of organizational democracy in the professional world. When Sophie joined her new corporation, she was enthusiastic and motivated about her new career direction. At this stage of the Percentile Theory, Sophie is known to have 100% of her enthusiasm for her new job and a strong commitment to excel as shown below:

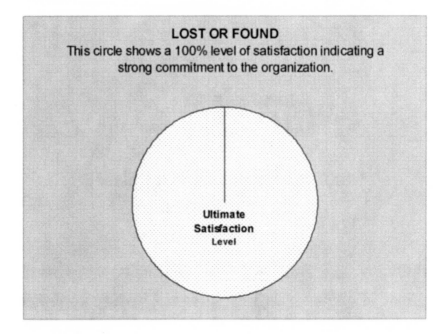

A complete circle equates to a 100% satisfaction level. This is the percentile level at which, most new employees join corporations when offered jobs they truly aspire for. The percentile level mostly applies to jobs people truly have a desire for and a true willingness to obtain. These jobs come with excitement, a high sense of fulfillment, and present the employee with a personal desire to excel in the field. The 100% percentile circle also indicates the level of commitment a new hire brings to the organization, a new member to church, a relationship or an engagement of any kind. The circle shows the level of Sophie's completeness when she took her new job.

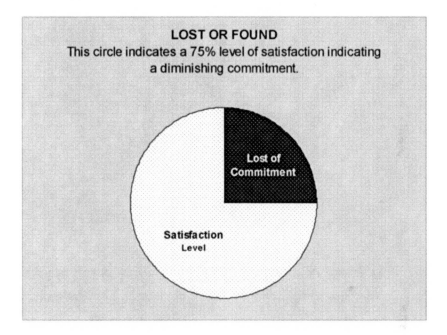

Sophie was pleased with her development and career success and loved her job until she started experiencing the realities of organizational psychology, nibbling and politics. Each negative experience by Sophie diminished her level of commitment to her company. Her education did not prepare her for the delicate and highly stressful situations that could be experienced in the business world. Unfavorable real-life experiences that bite away the sense-of-self of individuals and make them feel less worthy than they should, is typically the commencement of the nibbling of one's percentile circle as noted in the percentile theory. The above circle shows Sophie at a 75% commitment/satisfaction level.

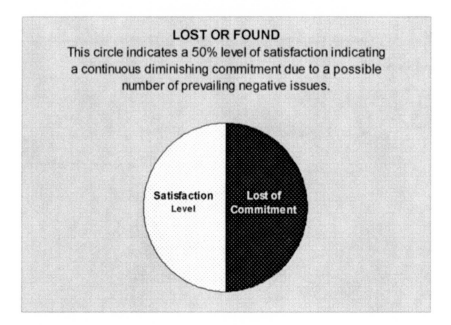

LOST OR FOUND
This circle indicates a 50% level of satisfaction indicating a continuous diminishing commitment due to a possible number of prevailing negative issues.

Sophie as reflected above is at a 50% commitment/satisfaction level due to prevailing negative experiences. Yet she continues to report to work steadily like she did when she joined the company. Her productivity and overall efficiency at this point suffers and drops considerably.

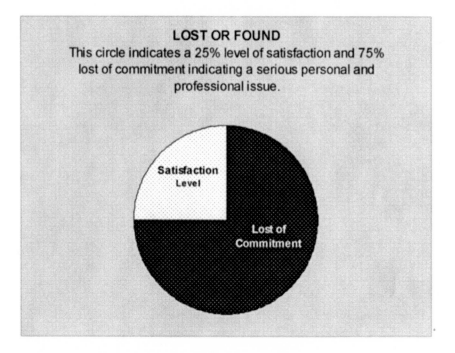

LOST OR FOUND
This circle indicates a 25% level of satisfaction and 75% lost of commitment indicating a serious personal and professional issue.

Sophie as reflected above is in an explosive state of complete dissatisfaction with both her job and sometimes her personal life. This is a stage where it becomes difficult to balance one's personal and professional lives as the low level of commitment/satisfaction impacts both lives. The obvious intricacies of organizational nibbling have taken a great toll. At this condition, the iconic state of the employee is "Lost" and he or she becomes overwhelmed with an unchangeable state of helplessness that could endanger others.

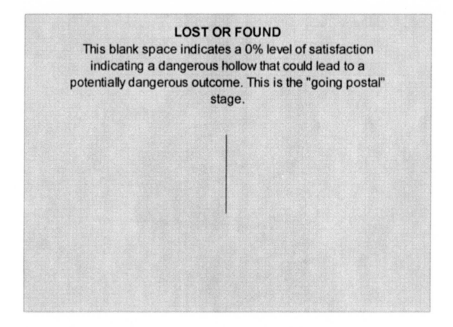

This is the "going postal" state. Dangerous and scary for both the employee and the organization, it is difficult to get out of this hemorrhagic state, filled with suicidal tendencies. This state requires a transformational inquest to avoid personal or workplace violence.

SOPHIE'S "LOST OR FOUND" CIRCLES

As shown below in the consolidated box of Sophie's depreciating circles are the stages individuals go through to being "Lost" and de-motivated at work or in their personal lives and/or relationships. It is important to find ways to avoid getting on the road to the suicidal state of complete hollowness.

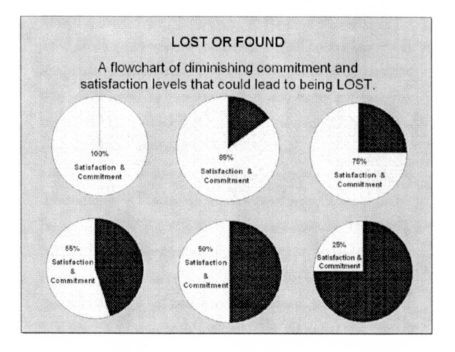

IMPORTANT NOTATION OF SOPHIE'S CIRCLE

Sophie loved her job and was pleased with her development and career success until she started experiencing the realities of negative organizational psychology and politics. With limited experience of the intricacies of organizational nibbling, Sophie lacked the ability or skills to fill back her commitment circle.

The Percentile Theory is an in-depth analysis of the gradual exploration and ultimate breakdown of individuals personally or professionally, based on their experiences within corporations, churches, personal relationships, and/or other contractual affiliations.

The theory covers the systematic depletion of a person's commitment level and enthusiasm that eventually leaves

one's circle of completeness hollow over time, thereby making him or her to function as an empty shell with little or no instinct or desire to maintain his or her job, remain in a relationship or continue to live. With each unfavorable experience, an individual loses percentages of his or her self-pride, commitment to a relationship or project and the enthusiasm to continue in a specific engagement regardless of the contractual agreement. This gradual intentional or non-intentional erosion of the employee's hope, pride, commitment, level of joy, satisfaction and/or interest in a relationship is what (a) leads to the breakdown of lives, (b) increases stress levels, (c) increases suicidal tendencies, and (d) violent actions such as murder or "going postal."

SOPHIE'S SITUATION

As noted in the case of Sophie, it all started with her teammates and supervisors who tested her frequently by making jokes and assigning tasks with dead end results as an assimilation process. Testing within organizational settings is prevalent and often seen as a procedural indoctrination into the business world, more specifically into high achieving departments. What has not been clearly researched and analyzed however, is that each unfavorable experience simply nibbles at the commitment level of the employee if unchecked. With Sophie, each negative experience in her new position took a few percentages off the commitment and self-pride she brought to the company. As indicated by Sophie's circles above, this example is one among many. Some companies may have hidden expectations not often disclosed to new hires during the interview process, some may have very poor leadership systems that very quickly diminishes the passion of new hires and some may even have poorly defined expectations that could lead to aggressive erosion of the commitment of staff to the corporation.

VALUES OF EMPOWERMENT

The percentile circle analogy showed that Sophie, within months, lost her desires, passion, and commitment to the new company due to the basket of negative experiences she had within a short span of getting hired. Sometimes, corporations, churches, relationships or whatever requires a high level of commitment have growing expectations. What is often forgotten is that the commitment of a person only rises when there is a mutual reward system. It could be as simple as:

- Continuous recognition;
- Positive reinvention to raise challenge levels;
- Ensuring a sense of belonging;
- Liberating them from fears through positive means;
- Shining lights on their actions;
- Recognizing their brilliancy regardless of its moderation;
- Giving them a sense of involvement;
- Granting some level of decision making;
- Helping to address areas of inadequacy;
- Celebrating milestones based on individual levels;
- Effective coaching and mentoring;

- Assisting with prevailing changes among others.

Sophie joined her corporation with 100% of her self-pride, commitment level, and an unquestionable enthusiasm. 60 days into her employment, unfavorable work experiences reduced her circle from 100% to 75%. The effect of the percentile theory could be daunting and anyone and everyone can be affected. Regardless of wealth, status, fame, educational achievement, political success or personality affiliation, all is susceptible to the effect of percentile nibbling. Realistically, Sophie wanted to fit in with her new team and accepted all tasks and responsibilities thrown at her. With time, she reluctantly accepted and eventually established a relationship with her team under a poorly managed corporation with unskilled bosses. Despite her extensive theoretical team-oriented knowledge, she was not quite ready for the complexities of the corporate world in a poorly managed system.

Millions of individuals like Sophie exist today. They have been drained by poor management policies or personal life experiences coupled with their unwillingness to embrace change and accept responsibility for some of their actions.

Some employees show up to work everyday like regular staff but have no commitment to the company, possess no enthusiasm and give the barest minimum. They practice the concept of limited-productivity-attendance or presenteeism. They engage themselves in activities of personal interest. This is Sophie's state. She joined her company as an enthusiastic new hire with a 100%

readiness level and commitment, with time she was nibbled to a point of no commitment.

Today, as she hangs, dangling on the side of the Golden Gate Bridge in her effort to commit suicide by leaping off the bridge, people are gasping for breath in reaction to every dangle. They are sighing in disbelief. Some are shedding tears of concern, sorrow and fear that it may be the end for Sophie. Most can't stop wondering how a person with much zeal and dedication to live and a job she cherished can degenerate to a level of such hollowness, from the effect of percentile nibbling.

This may seem extreme in descriptive sense but for those that have gone postal and with the increasing number of those that deliberate on quitting their jobs daily because of bad management principles, poor leadership, bad bosses, or personal inability to embrace change, it is important for you as a person to realize that you must take control of your life and not allow external factors from personal or professional settings to send you to the brink of giving up on everything. This book hopefully will help you fill back your nibbled circle of commitment and satisfaction.

ACTORS/ACTRESSES/SPORT ATHLETES/OTHERS

Renowned executive professionals, mayors, governors, athletes, artists, and various other famous individuals have been known to experience periods of downturns and breakdowns in their lives. These are called career doom-loops. This occurs when a once highly sought after star, athlete or notable person suddenly loses his or her demand for some time, and struggles to make ends meet. Those times of valley-periods or doom loops could lead to illnesses such as depressions, high-level stress, addiction, suicidal attempts, insanity, or completely unexpected acts by otherwise previously normal individuals. Sometimes, it could culminate in suicide. These unfavorable life experiences are an aggregate result of something I have termed the percentile effect. While most individuals deal with percentile nibbling in their varied ways, it is important to note that one is not required to stay in a "valley position or doom loop" if alternatives exist, regardless of how abstractly un-enticing the options may be.

CHAPTER 9

PERCENTILE THEORY RESEARCH STUDY

My five-year long-range research on being Lost or Found, and its relationship to leadership in the workplace, discovered a connection between male and female leadership and the percentile analysis.   Over 1500 professionals were interviewed and asked to respond to a survey on being Lost or Found and the reasons why.   Of those surveyed, 66% were women and 34% men.   The survey findings and unedited comments by some participants are presented.

Lost or Found: The Research

As noted in Chapter one, the research found that over 62% of the people interviewed were Lost. 12% were noted as the "Shiftless" group who were to an extent devoid of ambition or purpose but were not completely Lost. 26% were Found. This alarming finding led to an expansion of the research to find out why so many individuals felt Lost, especially in their jobs. The follow-up research culminated in the design and use of the following questionnaire and findings. The research findings showed that 46.5% of those surveyed prefer a male boss. 34.5% responded that it didn't matter if it was male or female and 19% claimed preference for a female boss. Most of the responses below were unedited unless when considered offensive.

1. Would you rather have a male or female boss?

Male (M)	Female (F)	Doesn't Matter/Optional	Total People	Ratio M/F
704	287	521	1512	M - 514
46.56%	18.96%	34.48%	100%	F - 998

2. Why? Give at least three key points. Be candid. This is confidential.

- Men are less emotional.

- Women are often too interested in getting to the top & don't care how they do it.

- Females are more intelligent and no chance of sex becoming an issue.

- I have never worked for a female. Females are rare in the technical environment I have worked in.

- Female bosses may be overly sympathetic to poor performers.

- I do not respect female authority because emotions and PMS suck to deal with.

- Males are not in competition with me.

- Males do not attempt to oppress my career goals.

- Female bosses are more people oriented.

- Females are easier to communicate with.

- Females are more manipulative and it's easier to get away with stuff.

- Male bosses have higher authority levels in the organization.

- Male bosses are willing to challenge unjust policies.

- Women and Men have different perspectives when dealing with commitments and timelines.

- While women are better listeners, they continue to listen when they don't understand.

- Most males are not "touchy-feely."

- Females have increased sensitivity and understanding.

- Males are level headed, consistent and don't have hormonal responses.

- Female bosses tend to be very territorial which can inhibit growth potential.

- Sometimes guys are more uncomfortable talking to a woman. This gives the woman an edge to speak and feel like she's listened to.

- Men can better sense my needs and are less cocky. I guess I am skilled at using them to my benefit.

- A female has most likely worked harder to get to the supervisory position, so she is more aware of the organizational bureaucratic rubbish.

- Women have more to lose if they make mistakes; therefore, they tend to read most reports twice… how frustrating.

- A female feels less obligated to her drinking buddies at work.

- Females have been more organized and willing to help me in my professional development.

- Females have a better understanding with general issues and they understand women's sicknesses.

- Male supervisors tend to be more business-oriented than women.

- Women are more nitpicky with details of a project(s).

3. **What gives you the most frustration at work? Give at least three key points.**

- People or managers who wait until the last minute to assign projects.

- Managers who do not go to bat for their employees.

- Unequal treatment of employees by managers

- Managers who keep valuable information to themselves.

- Trying to understand what motivates a poor performer (from a Supervisors perspective).

- Not having too high expectations for people I supervise…I guess this is my fault. Is it?

- People who won't pull their weight (lazy people).

- Not being recognized for an exceptional effort

- "Rule by Fear" management and in the box thinking.

- Bosses that don't have vision or control in their organization.

- Peers/Others that back stab to make themselves look good.

- Good Ole-Boy network systems.

- Micro Management and pushy bosses.

- When bosses talk down to people or are disrespectful toward creativity.

- When bosses/peers yell at employees in front of other employees.

- Plans of action to resolve problems from people who don't fully understand the symptoms.

- People who let problems escalate to panic mode before asking for help.

- Lack of Leadership or effective communication.

- Lack of process and procedures in place.

- Company policies that are not structured.

- Supervisor takes credit without sharing the praise with the department.

- No support system in place to create an environment that promotes new levels of achievement.

- A boss with no people skills/interpersonal skills.

- Lack of work to do or boredom.

- Unethical managers and unfair labor practices.

- Too many Chiefs and not enough Indians.

4. What gives you the greatest satisfaction at work? State at least two points.

- Accomplishing a team goal, especially when the team has worked well together.

- Finishing a project before the deadline.

- Figuring out a new software program (or process) by myself.

- Complimenting people for work completed beyond expectations.

- Monetary reward for hard work.

- Bosses that support my career goals.

- A staff that appreciates my leadership style and contributions.

- Giving people the encouragement and promotions that they deserve.

- Being viewed as a valuable contributor.

- True appreciation from people who recognize your hard work.

- Having people you can count on to get the job done.

- Constructive feedback.

- Challenging assignments.

- When I'm confronted with a problem no one can figure out and I can resolve it.

- Teaching others how to troubleshoot problems and displaying a knack for being successful.

- Perks to boost up employees motivation.

- Good work ethics and value teamwork.

- Exceeding profit goals.

- The support and guidance of my peers and management.

- Knowing my team appreciates me and we are able to understand each others role in the workplace.

- Career advancement/Promotion.

- Positive attitudes of co-workers.

- Strong morale.

- Advancement opportunities and job security.

- Meeting colleagues and new friends.

As noted by the comments above and in the overall analysis of the four-question survey, the most common areas of concerns were:

1. Poor management

2. Unfavorable work environment

3. Significant gap between expectation and reality

4. Unclear goals on the part of the employee and management

5. Unhealthy personal/professional relationships

6. Incompatibility

7. Poor structure of reward systems

8. Lack of understanding of what motivates employees

Your immortality will be best determined by the positive
influence you create on the life of others especially when
such actions were equally difficult for you

Sylvester Fadal

CHAPTER 10

LEADERSHIP/WORK SATISFACTION/SELF EMPOWERMENT

There has been extensive research conducted on the subject of empowerment, work satisfaction, and leadership. This is perhaps one of the most researched areas by graduate students and independent consultants. Despite the extensive findings and recommendations layered all over libraries across the world, some employers chose to ignore the values of these findings. Their non-willingness to embrace these important, productivity building strategies are some of the reasons why employees continue to practice extensive "presenteeism" at work.

Some employers believe absenteeism is the only problem they face but reality is, it is easier to track those that fail to show up to work than those that religiously show up as planned but give very little in terms of productivity to the corporation.

Some of these employees based on my research use their work environments to achieve other personal goals beside the work they are paid to perform.

They take online classes, do their homework at work, conduct online shopping, and plan their weddings and/ or other personal activities. Some have even mastered the act of managing independent personal business from the location of their employers. This is all orchestrated by a complete lack of commitment to the corporation they are trapped in. These set of employees simply wait for the opportunity to jump to a new corporation that would value and treat them better.

IS YOUR BOSS THE PROBLEM?

There is no question that corporations are filled with unqualified management staff. Be that as it may, it is easier to blame individual problems at work on bad bosses.

Deep down within, it is important to always ask the question, if your boss was changed today, would your problems and concerns suddenly go away?

Not exactly as indicated by several research findings. However, there are bad bosses out there and research indicates that many employees have thought of resigning from their positions due to bad bosses.

Do we have bad bosses at work? Absolutely. The reality is, bad bosses are not the primary reasons why people develop stress at work or lose their commitment and dedication to a company. Perhaps some of the strongest drivers of work stress are the inability to develop an effective strategy of dealing with the complexities of the professional environment, up to and including (a) dealing with a bad or good boss for that matter, (b) handling the complex policies of the organization, (c) dealing with the multitudes of attitudes and habits of coworkers and accepting change as it comes.

WHAT ARE YOUR OPTIONS?

In our complex world, environmental influences impact our actions. The new millennium era further encourages wild acts, unchecked extreme mind-sets and embracement of immorality, and poor attitude at the core. Be that as it may, we must not allow these magnitudes of environmental complexities to control our person and influence us from the "Found" column to being "Lost." In my drive to gain ongoing satisfaction, I developed five simple rules of personal satisfaction and engagement as noted below.

Rules of Self Satisfaction and Engagement

1. Love yourself & family unconditionally

2. Be grateful for each day and enjoy it to the fullest

3. Hold no grudges (through a conscious effort)

4. Embrace change

5. Have a Personal time

In my dissertation research conducted in 2003 on Fortune 500 corporations with a synopsis published by the American Society for Training and Development (ASTD) in 2004, a journal read by consultants, managers, trainers, and executives worldwide, I found that the cornerstone to building and maintaining successful and growing organizations and team management successes was effective leadership on the part of executives, managers, teams, and project leaders.

In addition, my research findings revealed that the commonality between all the literature and books I studied was that:

> **Leadership is the most integral architect that underlies the effectiveness of teams, alongside other factors such as employee empowerment programs. No matter the efforts put in by employees or the number of attempts made by companies to establish and organize teams, if there are no commensurate qualified leaders who meet all the fundamental criteria needed for success, the efforts are either bound to fail or have limited impact.**

CIRCLE OF FRIENDS

The commonality between this book, most empirical literature, and my upcoming book shows that a balance of good leadership, friendship, relationship and companionship is the most essential structural design that underlies the effectiveness, confidence and success of individuals personally and professionally. No matter the efforts put in by people or the number of attempts made by psychologists, counselors and support teams to transform a person, if the individual has not developed an innate desire to improve and change, accompanied by commensurate positive actions to reengineer his or her life, no change will happen. The circle of one's personal and professional friends speaks volumes in transitioning from a "Lost" to a "Found" person.

Great moral philosophers often agree that no magic "manual" catalogs answers for complex life dilemmas. It is important not to expect one. If one's action is intended to bring about results that will benefit a significant number of people, it falls into the Utilitarian model. In line with this model, this book is intended to provide the greater good to most individuals like yourself and others that may find it relatively valuable to moderating and improving their complex lives. Hopefully, applying some of the recommendations in this book may assist you in dealing with some form of nibbling on your person.

Societies, especially capitalist societies, encourage a complex connectivity between leadership and management, all for business optimization reasons. There is nothing wrong with the desires of corporations or individuals to make money. What is wrong however is the usage of human resources as procedural tools or property towards meeting those goals without regard to how those actions impact the lives of the people over time.

Great leaders and corporations must truly care about creating a balanced relationship between corporate growth and individual enrichment. Every year, Fortune.com outlines the list of best corporations. The list does serve as a valuable resource tool for individuals seeking to work in corporations that recognize and value their staff. Any corporation that has some of the key leadership traits below, based on feedback gathered from my survey is perhaps worth joining.

Positive Leadership Traits –
Developer
Innovator
Visionary
Driver
Passionate
Integrity/Honest
Self-Confident
Cognitive Skills
Motivator
High Self-Awareness
Balanced-Oriented
Mission-Driven
Communicator
Change Agent
Challenge Status Quo

Independent

High Influencer

NEW WORLD ERA

Organizations and people are entering a period of tremendous competition and change in all walks of life regardless of one's career path, daily activities, or what is viewed as a common symbiotic need. As a person, be ready and willing to embrace that change and devise a chock-full of ways to maintain a level of satisfaction for your personal growth and well being. The origin of "Lost" or "Found" and the "Percentile Theory" has a direct link to leadership and the ways individuals are managed in their personal and professional lives.

Empowerment that was once seen as a strong tool in building the commitment levels of professionals at work is starting to lose its importance to corporations. Despite the inroads made by organizations in empowering employees in the last 30 years, it is perhaps most important to you as a person to find a career, an environment, a corporation or an independent business that will bring you the most satisfaction in life. In the overall scheme of things, learn to avoid situations that make you less of yourself and recognize that when you embrace the positive things in your life and develop a "Found" attitude, it may stop you from heading down the road of Sophie Duze.

FINAL THOUGHT

Sometimes, complex everyday life experiences can be overwhelming. The energy to cope could get lost. No matter how difficult it gets, our approach to the situation matters most. When everything fails, strive to continue to do the best. Maintain a modicum of hope. At least that is what truly matters.

The End

EXHIBIT 1

LOST OR FOUND SURVEY

Self-Assessment/Questionnaire

#	Core Satisfaction Factors	Yes (X)	No (X)
1	I am action oriented		
2	My job is satisfying		
3	I seek the comfort zone		
4	I sometimes have a high level of absenteeism		
5	I communicate effectively		
6	I have a good sense of humor		
7	I am in control of my career		
8	I am approachable		
9	I always seek completion		
10	I am a visionary person		
11	I appreciate diversity		
12	I can learn on the fly		
13	Trustworthy could be used to describe me		
14	Perseverance is synonymous with me		
15	Sometimes I sweat the little things		
16	Sometimes I can be combative		
17	I have a good work and life balance		
18	I have a great attitude		
19	I work best in teams		
20	I tend to be self-motivating		
21	I sometimes get complacent		
22	My fears sometimes control me		
23	I have a great circle of friends		
24	I embrace new challenges		
25	I have strong problem solving skills		
26	I make effective decisions under stress		
27	My technical knowledge is up-to-date		
28	I am a change agent		
29	My life is full of ambiguity		
30	My boss is responsible for my satisfaction at work		
	Subtotal		
	Adjusted Total		
	Grand Total		

Calculation of Points

Subtotal:

1) Assign 2 points for each "Yes" response and add up the total in the "Yes" column.

2) Assign 1 point for each "No" response and add up the total in the "No" column.

Adjusted Total:

3) If you answered, "Yes" to the following questions: (#s 3, 4, 16, 22, 29, 30) deduct 2 points each from the Subtotal in the "Yes" column.

4) If you answered, "No" to questions: (#s 3, 4, 16, 22, 29, 30) add 1 point for each to the Subtotal in the "No" column.

Grand Total:

5) Now, add the Adjusted Total in the "Yes" and "No" column to get the Grand Total and refer to the Lost or Found Rankings below.

Lost or Found Ranking
(Found= 50 and higher; Grey Zone/Shiftless= 49-45; **Lost= 44 and below** (Most "Shiftless" are likely to end up being "Lost" unless a Critical Intervention occurs)

About The Author

Dr. Sylvester Fadal embraced business optimization and efficiency building within corporations, years ago. His published doctoral dissertation study on Fortune 500 corporations titled "Employee Empowerment as a Business Optimization Strategy" was widely received by training and organizational development professionals. A synopsis of his findings was published by the American Society for Training and Development. Dr. Fadal was invited to speak by various refereed journals and institutions on the subject of performance optimization, organizational capacity building, efficiency and productivity and individual growth.

As a professor of business he has shared the information in this book with his students for almost 10 years. With a strong passion for the world's disadvantaged that lead to the formation of Fadal & Associates 501 © 3 non-profit that reaches out to low income individuals in the greater Bay Area and Africa, he continues to galvanize support for the world's poorest people.

His goals are spiritual, family and philanthropy. Some proceeds from this book will be used to support his not-for-profit foundation that seek to feed the poor and open doors to those whose lives are being destroyed by AIDS, poverty, child slavery, abandonment and starvation among others. A stronger act of kindness is to give to those that can't give back.

Dr. Fadal is married with three children and resides in Northern California, USA.

Printed in the United States
136768LV00006BA/52/P